A KID'S GUIDE TO FEELINGS
FEELING HAPPY

BY KIRSTY HOLMES

KidHaven
PUBLISHING

Published in 2019 by KidHaven Publishing, an Imprint of Greenhaven Publishing, LLC
353 3rd Avenue, Suite 255, New York, NY 10010

Written by: Kirsty Holmes
Edited by: Holly Duhig
Designed by: Danielle Rippengill

Cataloging-in-Publication Data

Names: Holmes, Kirsty.
Title: Feeling happy / Kirsty Holmes.
Description: New York : KidHaven Publishing, 2019. | Series: A kid's guide to feelings | Includes glossary and index.
Identifiers: ISBN 9781534526808 (pbk.) | ISBN 9781534526792 (library bound) | ISBN 9781534526815 (6 pack)
Subjects: LCSH: Happiness--Juvenile literature. | Emotions--Juvenile literature.
Classification: LCC BF575.H27 H645 2019 | DDC 152.4'2--dc23

*Image Credits: All images are courtesy of Shutterstock.com, unless otherwise specified.
With thanks to Getty Images, Thinkstock Photo and iStockphoto. Front Cover – MarinaMay,
yayasya, jirawat phueksriphan, Piotr Urakau, Samuel Borges Photography, Rawpixel.com,
Kobsoft, Sergiy Bykhunenko. Images used on every page – MarinaMay, yayasya, Piotr Urakau.
2 – Strix, Sudowoodo. 5 – Frame Studio, Andrii Symonenko, Sudowoodo. 6 – Makc, Andrii Symonenko,
Sudowood. 7 – Strix. 8 – Rawpixel.com, Maryna Kulchytska, TinnaPong. 9 – Daxiao Productions,
VaLiza, travelview, Rawpixel.com. 11 – Mark Nazh, Africa Studio, naluwan. 12 – Samuel Borges Photography,
ViChizh. 12 & 13 – Evellean. 13 – ColorBolt. 14 – gst, Khomenko Serhii, Strix. 15 – espies, Billion Photos,
3445128471. 16 – aliaksei kruhlenia. 17 – Luis Louro. 18 – KK Tan. 19 – Strix. 21 – Elena Nichizhenova,
Rawpixel.com, 5 second Studio, VaLiza. 22 & 23 – Sudowoodo, Andrii Symonenko.*

Printed in the United States of America

CPSIA compliance information: Batch # BS18KL: For further information contact Greenhaven Publishing LLC, New York, New York at 1-844-317-7404.

CONTENTS

Words that look like **this** can be found in the glossary on page 24.

We all have **emotions**, or feelings, all the time. Our feelings are very important. They help us think about the world around us, and know how we want to **react**.

Sometimes, we feel good. Other times, we feel bad.

Captain Cheerful loves to play with Cocoa the cat. Captain Cheerful is feeling really happy.

Let's find out more…

HOW DO WE FEEL WHEN WE'RE HAPPY?

You might feel really relaxed…

…you might feel warm all over…

…or you might feel like your chest or belly is really full.

8

HOW DO WE LOOK
WHEN WE'RE HAPPY?

You can tell someone is happy because they might…

…jump around…

…or dance around…

This is called **body language**.

…or they might be laughing and smiling.

WHY DO WE FEEL HAPPY?

FEELING HAPPY IS AN IMPORTANT EMOTION.

Human beings live together in a society. Everyone has a part to play.

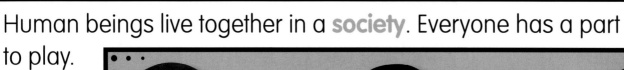

We all want to do different things.

WHEN I GROW UP...
DOCTOR
SCIENTIST
ASTRONAUT

12

SING! EXPLORE!

When we feel happy, we feel good.

If we feel happy doing something, we want to do it more. We also get better at doing it.

KNOWING WHAT MAKES US FEEL HAPPY HELPS US KNOW WHAT WE WANT TO DO.

THINGS THAT MAKE US HAPPY

LOVED ONES!

MUSIC!

FAVORITE THINGS!

WHEN FEELING HAPPY IS GOOD

Feeling happy is a great feeling. It can help us to know when things w are doing, or people in our lives, are good for us.

When we are happy, others around us will feel happy, too. This can mean we make lots of new friends, and help others.

WHEN FEELING HAPPY IS BAD

Feeling happy doesn't always tell us something is good for us.

Too much of a good thing can be **unhealthy**.

Some things can make us feel good, but are actually bad for us.

Feeling happy is great. But you should always listen to your other emotions, too. Pretending to be happy when you are not is a bad idea.

Listen to all of your emotions. 19

DEALING WITH FEELINGS

Captain Cheerful can share her happiness.
Agents of F.E.E.L.S: GO!

If you are feeling happy…

…sharing your happiness with others…

…can make you feel even happier!

It's OK to feel sad, too... but it's nice to feel better afterwards!

THE END 23

GLOSSARY

ACHIEVE	get something by trying hard
BODY LANGUAGE	things a person does with their body that tell you how they feel
EMOTIONS	a strong feeling such as joy, hate, sadness, or fear
INFECTIOUS	easily spread around
REACT	act or respond to something that has happened or been done
RELAXED	calm and not tense
ROSY	deep pink in color
SOCIETY	a collection of people living together in a group
UNHEALTHY	harmful to your health

INDEX